Y0-CAS-978

the organized ᗷride's *thank you note* handbook

the organized Bride's thank you note handbook

Let Systems and **101** Modern Sample
Thank You Notes Take You From
Overwhelmed to Organized

Stacey Agin Murray

ORGANIZED Artistry PRESS

The Organized Bride's Thank You Note Handbook

*Let Systems and 101 Modern Sample Thank You Notes
Take You from Overwhelmed to Organized*

Copyright © 2014 by Stacey Agin Murray. All rights reserved.

No part of this book may be used or reproduced in any manner
whatsoever without written permission except in the case of brief
quotations embodied in critical articles and review.

For more information, please contact
Stacey Agin Murray
Organized Artistry, LLC
PO Box 2682, Fair Lawn, NJ 07410
(201) 703–8438
stacey@organizedartistry.com

ISBN 978-0-9815175-1-3

Book Design: Peri Poloni-Gabriel,
Knockout Design, www.knockoutbooks.com

Acknowledgments

I couldn't write a book about saying "thank you" without thanking those who got me here in the first place. Without the ideas, knowledge, love, and support of the following people, this book would still be in the back of my file cabinet.

I'd like to thank the recent brides who peer-reviewed my manuscript: Elana DeBartolo Faugno, Shira Price Marshall, and Julie Simmons. Your comments and insights strengthened the manuscript and opened my eyes to the needs of a variety of brides.

A thank you also goes to those who led me to these ladies: Kathi Evans of All the Best Weddings and Celebrations, Penny Cohen, and Debbie Stanley.

A hearty thank you goes to Linda Samuels of Oh, So Organized! for reading my manuscript and offering me her time and writing/publishing words of wisdom. You took the journey to authorship before me, and I have learned more from you than you can imagine. A big, "organized" thank you goes to Debbie Stanley and the NAPO Authorship and Publishing Special Interest Group for keeping me accountable for my progress and encouraging me to reach the writing and publishing finish line. For her friendship and never-ending support of my writing, a huge thank you goes to Ellen Palestine of Finally Organized!.

To my book coach, Maggie Lichtenberg of Publishing Options, thank you for putting me to work to make this book a reality. Without your knowledge and guidance, I'd still have a book without a title. To my copy editor Stefanie Lazer and managing editor Suzanne Murray of StyleMatters Writing Services, thank you for fleshing out my words and ideas so they could sing their song so sweetly. Your enthusiasm for my manuscript and commitment to the project (despite all the snowstorms!) kept me focused and feeling confident that I could reach my goal. To Peri Poloni-Gabriel of Knockout Design, I cannot thank you enough for lending your years of experience, design intuition, and creativity to the design of the cover and interior of my book. Your talents have turned my words into a work of art.

To my parents, Millie and Gerry Agin, thank you for recognizing my flair for the written word and always encouraging me to write. Your file cabinet is filled with my writing; now you have something you can put on the shelf! To my husband, Jay, our thank you note writing experience was the inspiration for this book. From the moment I told you I was going to write a book, you have been supportive; you believed in me when I wasn't sure I could make it happen, and you have held my hand throughout the entire process. For all that and then some...thank you.

Table of Contents

List of Appendixes

Introduction

Think back to when you were young. You would receive a gift and, just like your parents taught you, you were polite and said, "Thank you." But, according to Mom, you also had to write a thank you note. You may have been allowed to sign an old finger painting from kindergarten in lieu of a formal note. People thought that was totally adorable, didn't they?

Bride-to-be, you're not in kindergarten anymore. Finger paintings won't cut it.

You're in the big leagues now. Engraved stationery. Note cards with "Mr. & Mrs." printed on the front. Envelope liners. Wedding thank you notes are much scarier stuff than finger paint.

Even scarier than the fancy note cards is the magnitude of the project you are about to embark upon. Picking out china is the easy part. Thanking everyone for it is more of a challenge. No finger paintings are allowed.

This is probably one of the few times in your life that you will be blessed with an inordinate amount of gifts—engagement gifts, shower gifts, gifts from ethnic ceremonies, and the daddy of them all: wedding gifts! Friends and relatives are spending money so you and your future spouse will be able to elegantly cook and serve meals, have towels for every bathroom and linens for every bedroom, and put some money in the bank, too. These generous gift givers have taken the time to shop for you and attend your nuptial-related events. In turn, they deserve a thank you note that is written with them specifically in mind.

You may be asking yourself, "Do I have to take the time and energy to write a heartfelt and well-thought-out thank you note? Isn't it easier to write a generic note thanking people for their gift and for attending the engagement party/bridal shower/wedding?" Sure, it's easier. But is that the kind of note you would prefer to receive after putting time, money, and effort into purchasing a gift for someone?

Shortly after my husband and I got engaged, gifts began to pour in and pile high in our homes. I thought about how lucky we were to be blessed with thoughtful presents from our family and friends. I then began to consider the number of thank you notes my husband and I would be writing over the next year. I envisioned us as two haggard-looking newlyweds chained to the dining room table, hands trembling with exhaustion, tongues dry from licking envelopes (thank goodness for self-stick stamps!). I wondered, How will we keep our thank you notes fresh and original? How can we prevent a bad case of thank you note burnout? How can we stay organized?

Before we started writing the majority of our nuptial-related thank you notes, I looked to the library and bookstores for some ideas and guidance. What I found on the shelves were books filled with formal ways of saying thank you to formal people who gave formal gifts like silver teapots and chafing dishes. Some of the sample thank yous were reminiscent of the thank you notes that Elizabeth Taylor might have written after her wedding in the 1950 movie *Father of the Bride*. I chuckled my way through most of those books—they were much more entertaining than they were helpful. I thought to myself, "We can't write thank you notes that sound like that! We'll get laughed at!"

I needed a plan. I knew that this task would require a high level of motivation and organization. To stay focused and on task, I would have to create a system—one that would be easy to follow yet meet the demands of the job ahead of us.

Using a shred of wrapping paper and a purple pen, I jotted down a few ideas about what makes a thank you note good or bad.

I split the paper in half and on the "bad" side, I noted characteristics of generic thank you notes I had received. Those notes had left me feeling empty inside and wondering why I ran all over the city to find the bride and groom the perfect gift. I once received a thank you note that read, "Thank you for your generous gift and for making our day so special." My guess is that the bride and groom used that line in all of their thank yous, never remembering that I had *not* attended their wedding! On the "good" half of my wrapping paper, I wrote about the thank you notes that had made me smile. Those were the ones in which the bride and groom, whether or not they knew me well, took the time to write a note meant only for me. I gazed at both sides of my piece of wrapping paper, and I knew which side represented the strategy my husband and I would pursue. After much thought, I created a seven-step system for writing personalized engagement, shower, and wedding gift thank you notes. It was designed to free us from the constant worry of "What do we write?" and instead organize our ideas and enable us to put our energies into writing creative, thoughtful, and heartfelt thank you notes.

In the end, my husband and I composed approximately 225 nuptial-related thank you notes. Soon after we had finished writing a sizeable number of them, I had the chance to attend a family get-together. Much to my surprise and delight, many of my relatives took me aside to thank me for the notes we had written to thank them for their shower and wedding gifts. They were impressed that I had written notes with them specifically in mind. They didn't comment on how they had received other thank you notes in less time. Once their note was in their hands, they recognized that we had taken the time to think of them as well as their thoughtful and generous gift. A personalized thank you note made them feel as if they were an important part of our marriage-related events. Little did I know that the system I had designed would produce so many of what I refer to as "crowd-pleasin'-puts-a-smile-on-their-face" thank you notes. More important, my mother received many phone calls from friends and relatives gushing about the thank you note they had received.

Many brides and grooms say they are unsure of what to write and feel this is an overwhelming task. But you have nothing to fear and much goodwill to gain when you approach this as something not just to get done but to do right!

This book will

- *alleviate the fears you may have regarding the thank you note writing process,*
- *provide you with a system that will help you to organize the thank you note writing process,*
- *help you compose thank you notes that will put smiles on the faces of the people who receive them,*
- *reveal the art of personalizing a thank you note and its advantages,*
- *offer tools and tips for staying organized during your thank you note writing experience, and*
- *provide 101 modern sample thank you notes for the busy bride and groom of the twenty-first century.*

Even if you are reading this after you've started writing your thank you notes, there is no time like the present to change your thank you note writing patterns. Follow the no-fail system presented here and

don't be surprised when people start thanking **YOU** for your thank you notes.

Writing Thank You Notes: Challenges and Solutions

When you were a kid, did you ever have a birthday party with balloons, games, cake, and presents? By the end of the afternoon, your home resembled a war zone and you had the time of your life!

A few days later, your mom probably came to you, note cards in hand, and said, "Time to write thank you notes! In your best handwriting, write about the gift you got and how much you liked it, even if you didn't like it. And don't forget to thank your friends for coming to your party."

You may have replied, "Aw, Mom! Do I have to?" You may have been thinking, "OK, maybe I don't need a party next year...."

Mom or Dad usually helped you write thank you notes when you were younger. No one expected more than two sentences from you—just about anything you wrote was acceptable. Now you're a grown-up and people have higher expectations. They expect at least three sentences, more legible handwriting, and no finger paintings. The pressure is on.

Why does writing thank you notes often make people anxious? High expectations, time constraints, performance anxiety, and knowledge of one's poor penmanship or mediocre writing skills all come into play when performing this sizeable task. One might stare at a blank card and think, "What should I write to my second cousins whom I see once a year?" "Will Aunt Shirley be able to read my chicken scratch?" "Will I be judged as a person by the content of my note?"

A thank you note is a reflection of you. It encompasses your reputation and character.

No one wants to feel inadequate, ashamed, or stressed during this exciting and often turbulent time. But, regardless of skill, one must rise to the occasion and say thank you to all who have been so generous (and even to those you think have not been so generous).

What Feelings Do Brides-to-Be Experience when Thinking about Writing Thank You Notes?

Fear

For many, thank you note writing can seem like a daunting task. Maybe even torture.

There is a little-known disease called "Thank-you-note-itis." You won't find it in any medical journal, but it has been known to produce a paralyzing fear in many people. The symptoms are easy to spot. Your hand begins to shake. You have an urge to cry at the sight of ecru stationery. You're convinced that returning all of the gifts would be easier than writing thank you notes for them.

Fears can be fueled by embarrassment.
Some fears are:

- ☞ *You have illegible handwriting that no one will be able to decipher.*

- ☞ *Your husband has illegible handwriting that no one will be able to decipher.*

- ☞ *You'll run out of your fancy "Mr. and Mrs." stationery and have to use different cards, tipping everyone off that you didn't order enough.*

- ☞ *Your cousins who chipped in on a gift will three-way conference call to compare their thank you notes.*

- ☞ *Everyone will bring your thank you notes to the next family BBQ and use them to keep the fire going.*

Procrastination

When it comes to thank you notes, procrastination is one of your worst enemies. It is a bad habit, plain and simple. When a task is troublesome or oppressive, it is easy to procrastinate, delaying the inevitable by postponing the task until a better day or time is found. One night you're out to dinner with friends, another night you're working late, next weekend you're out of town. Your favorite phrase becomes, "I'll get around to it." It's now six months later, relatives are calling your mother, your mother is calling you, and you're probably hiding in the closet, pen in hand, writing anything just to get everyone off your back.

A few reasons why brides-to-be procrastinate:

Feelings of inadequacy. You're probably not a professional writer—that's OK, most of us aren't. But if you asked a group of professional writers if they struggled with composing all of their wedding-related thank you notes, you might be surprised to hear more than a few of them say, "Yes."

The desire for perfection. We all have a vision in our heads of what "perfect" is. But the fear of not being able to make that vision a reality can sometimes get in the way of staying on task and meeting our goals. The perfect thank you note is the one that acknowledges a gift giver's generosity and shows gratitude.

A lack of organizing skills. Tracking hundreds of gifts and thank you notes requires a high level of organization and time management that not everyone is born with. Even the most organized bride-to-be can misplace an address, attach the wrong card to a gift, or forget to pick up more stamps.

Overwhelmed

Today's bride-to-be has a lot on her plate. She probably works full time. She may be relocating to a new city. She may even have children to take care of. On top of all of her everyday responsibilities, she has a new project: thank you cards. More often than not, it is an undertaking that lands in the lap of the bride.

Note: Because it is most common that a bride assumes the note writing responsibilities, this book has been written from that perspective. But the advice given is applicable to all, whether you're the bride or the groom. Everyone, whether male or female, is capable of writing a thoughtful, personalized, and well-organized thank you note.

Writing thank you notes does not have to cause fear, procrastination, and a feeling of being overwhelmed. Here are a few stress-reducing ideas that will keep you from buckling under the pressure and will help you move forward to complete the task.

SOLUTIONS:

Tips for a Positive Thank You Note Writing Experience

Visualize

Visualization is the ability to use our imagination to see images in our mind and make them come true. The brain is a powerful tool. It can get you through this task or it can turn it into a difficult process. Despite its capabilities, the brain cannot be programmed without you. You choose whether this task will be effortless or overwhelming. You have the power to tell your brain what to see and how to feel. Take a deep breath. Think positively.

Here are a few visualization choices for those stressful note-writing moments:

> ☞ *Visualize the pile of your thank you notes getting smaller.*

> ☞ *See yourself running across a finish line with completed thank you cards in hand.*

> ☞ *Picture yourself placing finished thank you notes in the mailbox.*

> ☞ *Imagine the smile on the face of the recipient reading your thank you note. (And there will be many smiles!)*

Practice

There's an old joke: One man says to another, "Excuse me. How do I get to Carnegie Hall?" And the other man says, "Practice, practice, practice!" It's also the way to write extraordinary thank you notes.

No one said you had to dive right into that box of pristine stationery. A blank page, even to the professional writer, can be an intimidating sight. Before you begin, allow yourself a few moments to prepare yourself and your supplies. These steps will save you time, aggravation, and the urgent need to order extra note cards:

Select a good pen. Use blue or black ink—any other color looks unsophisticated. Take one note card and practice using the pen on it. Does it glide across the tooth of the paper you've chosen? Does it leak and smudge? When you are happy with the way your pen of choice is working, buy three to five more of them. One may run out of ink. One may roll under your refrigerator. You need to be prepared.

The color of the pen used in the note should match the color of the pen used for the envelope's mailing address. Uniformity makes a clean visual statement. Although your words of thanks are the key component of your note, presentation is equally important. Using two different colored pens shows disorganization and a lack of regard for the art of thank you note writing.

Practice your penmanship. If you are taking the time to write a thank you note with an artistry that parallels that of a Shakespearean sonnet, you are going to want the recipient to be able to read it. Consider printing (instead of script) if you have handwriting that has been described as illegible by all who know and love you.

Think on scrap paper. Write on note cards. We used it for math tests and we can use it for thank you notes, too. How many times have you thought you knew what you wanted to write but you changed your mind halfway through? Writing your thank you message on scrap paper first will eliminate most grammatical and penmanship mistakes on your note card. Besides helping you to get your thoughts neatly written and in order, it's also an ingenious way to recycle the wrapping paper strewn across your living room.

Space out your text on the note card. If your handwriting tends to be on the large side and you often run out of room on greeting cards, my advice to you is practice before you waste a large number of expensive note cards. Cut scrap paper (recycle more wrapping paper) or find similarly sized, unlined index cards to duplicate the size of your note card. Using a ruler and pencil, create margins a minimum of a quarter inch around the top, bottom, and sides of the writing area. Make a few practice cards like these so you can practice writing both short and lengthy thank yous within the boundaries of the margins. When you feel you are ready to ditch the wrapping paper and index cards, start using the note cards. The layout of your note will look centered and skillfully designed.

Set Reasonable Goals

The key to avoiding thank you note burnout is to set reasonable goals. Setting unrealistic or unreasonable deadlines for yourself can set you up for failure. Telling yourself you're going to write twenty thank you cards a night might be OK for those who have a penchant for the pen. But for most people such a goal is often unattainable. Completing three to five thank you notes per sitting is often what couples try to accomplish in an evening.

You might think, "Well, I have one hundred thank you cards to write. If I do five to ten a night, I'll be done in less than two weeks!" If you can actually achieve that goal, you deserve a medal or you have an amazingly helpful husband. Chances are, you haven't answered your phone, gone through your mail, or stepped away from your writing table in those two weeks. You're about 30 thank you notes away from a wicked case of carpal tunnel syndrome.

This is where the phrase *know thyself* is important. If you know you have trouble sitting and writing for more than half an hour at a time, don't get down on yourself because you can't accomplish more in a day. Make that half hour a focused and productive one. If you know you need to take "brain breaks," try to write your thank yous every other day. If you're too pooped at night to write coherently, save your writing for the weekend, when you are better rested. Know thyself.

Thank you notes don't necessarily need to only be written at home at your dining room table. If you find yourself with a few moments to spare during your lunch hour or while waiting in line at the store,

- jot down thank you note ideas on a small notepad or in your favorite technological gadget
- e-mail ideas from your work computer to your home e-mail address
- bring cards with you to work if you can find somewhere quiet to think and write on your break or lunch hour

Even if you finish only one or two thank you notes while eating your lunch, that's one or two fewer cards you'll have to write tomorrow and one or two more people who will soon smile when they open their mailbox.

Establish Priorities

You may be thinking, "Where do I begin? Do I write thank you notes in alphabetical order? Write them to my family first? My husband's family? Or friends?"

The order in which you write your thank you notes is important to consider. Why? Think about the people from whom you have received gifts. Who is most likely to expect a thank you note in their mailbox ASAP? Is it your mother's friends from work? Your grandmother's eight brothers and sisters? Think about who wouldn't complain if they received your thank you note a little later. Your friends? Your second cousins on your father's side? Think about relatives that speak to each other often. You might want to mail their thank yous at the same time. You may also choose to send your thank you notes in the order in which the gifts arrived. Or you can do a combination of these: The first few gifts get the first thank you notes and, after that, start writing to elderly relatives or those who expect the fastest gift-to-thank-you turnaround. In the end, everyone's situation is different—you need to do whatever you feel is best for your particular circumstances.

Don't push off the inevitable—just do it. Think about all of the gifts you received, sit in a comfortable chair, and write to the best of your ability. As discussed earlier, procrastination only makes the situation worse. Even if you write just one thank you note on a night that you're tired or otherwise busy, it will bring you one step closer to your note-writing finish line. Make the note an easy one, like one to the friend from work who got you a cool clock or a relative you enjoy spending time with.

Work as a Team

Although this book focuses on the bride (let's face it, writing thank you notes usually ends up being the bride's responsibility), there is no reason why the groom, who benefits from all of these generous gifts too, can't do his share. He can seal envelopes while watching TV. He can stand in line for stamps at the post office. Given that he knows his friends and family better than you do, he can write thank you notes to them and add his personal touch—something every note should possess.

Assign tasks according to each person's strengths. If your handwriting is neater than your spouse's, you should consider doing the writing. If hubby works near a post office, it can be his job to get the stamps and mail the completed thank you notes. This is not the time to squabble over who does what. Marriage is about working as a team.

You've visualized, you've set reasonable goals, you've thought about priorities, and now you're ready to begin. It's time to tuck away your fears and preconceived notions about writing thank you notes.

No more procrastinating—you're about to get organized!

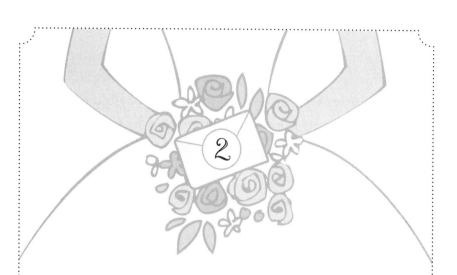

Let's Get Organized!

Picture this scenario: You and your significant other have cleared the table and are about to write thank you notes when you discover that the gift list is nowhere to be found. Three note cards have been mangled by the weight of the box they came in, and you can't find the pen you've used for the past week. You've already composed twenty-two thank you notes but neither of you can conceive of another exciting way to say, "Thanks for the _____ from our registry." You flip a coin to see who will thank

Aunt Tillie for her green crocheted afghan. You're biting your nails. Your spouse's eyes are glazing over. Another pen is found, an hour passes, and the only writing you've done is the address on Aunt Tillie's envelope. And now you're in no mood to write thank you notes.

Don't let this situation happen to you! One of the keys to making the thank you note writing process less stressful is to *be organized*. Being organized enables you to find and have what you need when you need it, whether it is brilliant words of thanks, pens that don't leak, or the time to write. It enhances productivity and promotes a feeling of order and peace of mind during an otherwise stressful time in one's life.

As a general rule, being organized also helps save you money, time, and stress. It sounds like a pretty generic statement, but let's take a look at how being disorganized could potentially affect (a) your money, (b) your time, and (c) your stress while composing thank you notes for engagement, bridal shower, and wedding gifts.

Being disorganized affects your money and can lead to
- *needing to pay to replace coffee-stained note cards*
- *having to repurchase misplaced pens and stamps*
- *loss of wages from part-time work or a freelance job*

Being disorganized affects your time and can lead to
- *having to search your home for pens and note cards*
- *sorting through scraps of paper to determine who gave you what gift*

✒ waiting in line at the post office because you don't know where you put those darn LOVE stamps

Being disorganized affects your money and time and can also lead to stress, such as

✒ arguing with your spouse about the money you had to spend to replace your note cards

✒ arguing with your spouse about the time you both wasted while in search of the gift list

✒ arguing with your spouse about the time you both wasted at the post office

And worst of all, what will your mother say when she finds out you haven't been writing your thank you notes because of your disorganization? And that you've been arguing with your new spouse! Enough said.

Organizing your thank you note writing process is the easiest way to successfully meet your thank you note writing goals. How can this be achieved? Follow these five basic organizing principles that will help guide you on your note-writing journey.

Five Basic Organizing Principles

Organizing Principle 1: *Group It All Together*

Think about it. If you kept your wedding dress on the back of your bedroom door, your headpiece in the living room, your veil in a box on your entertainment center, and your pantyhose in your sock drawer, what could potentially happen on your wedding day? If you said, "I may forget one of those things on the way to my ceremony!" you would be correct. If items that are used together for a specific purpose are not kept together, there is a good chance that one of those items may be lost or forgotten when you need it.

How does the principle of grouping it all together apply to writing thank you notes? By grouping all thank you note–related items in one place at all times, you will always know where to find them when you wish to start writing. If the items needed to write your thank you notes are spread around your home (or office or car) at the time you've set aside for writing, you will end up wasting a good deal of your writing time, which will then become searching time, which usually turns into aggravation time. And we all know that after aggravation time comes well-now-I'm-in-no-mood-to-write-thank-you-notes time.

Organizing Principle 2: *Use Containers*

A container is a receptacle for holding goods. It can be as simple as a shoebox or as ornate as a fancy leather bin from your local home store. Why bother to put your thank you note writing tools in a container if they're already grouped together? Two good reasons:

1. *The container creates an area that will safely store your writing products.*

2. *The container becomes a self-contained writing center that is easily transportable to your writing surface, whether it be a table, a lap desk, or another location.*

You can choose to place all of your writing tools (note cards, pens, scrap paper, gift list) in a large container or you can further divide them into subcontainers within the larger one. For example, note cards usually come in a box from the printer. Keep this box to house the note cards and matching envelopes so they don't get dirty or bent out of shape. Also, you can use a folder or clear plastic envelope to hold stamps, pens, and the lists of guests and other givers.

Once you've made decisions regarding containers, place your new self-contained writing center close to where you usually compose your thank yous. You'll never waste time looking for your note-writing materials again.

Organizing Principle 3: *Make an Appointment with Yourself*

We make appointments to have our hair cut, our teeth cleaned, and our health checked. If you're a busy person or know that *Procrastination* is your middle name, make an appointment with yourself for writing your thank you notes. With the exception of an emergency, you probably wouldn't consider canceling an appointment because you had too many errands to run or would prefer to sit home and watch TV. You would have to reschedule that appointment and possibly get hit with a cancellation fee. Although there's no cancellation fee for missing a night of note writing, assign your short-term thank you note writing career the same importance as you would self-care. Make sure to carve out the time—this task is just as essential as a doctor's appointment. But, before doing so, consider two things:

☛ *what time of day you work best and*

☛ *how long you can sit and write thank you notes before getting tired and antsy.*

*When considering the above items, ask yourself a
few questions:*

1. *How many days per week am I able to devote to this task?
   One? Two? Five, with weekends off?*
2. *What is my attention span like? How long am I able to give
   my full attention to this task per day? Two hours? An hour?
   Fifteen minutes?*
3. *When do I have the most energy for writing and being
   creative? Midday? Evening? Weekends?*

The answers to these questions will help you determine the best days and times to write. Be honest with yourself when answering the above questions. Don't try to sit and write for two hours if you know your limit is a half hour—you'll only waste time and be upset with yourself when you're not as productive as you had planned to be. Have your spouse ask himself the same questions.

This task must be completed and will take high priority for a while. The thank you cards must be written and mailed in a timely manner. Block out the time on your calendar. Don't allow yourself to schedule anything else during that time. If you make it a priority and treat it like a true appointment, you'll be more likely to keep it.

Organizing Principle 4: *Break It Down*

Would you ever consider sitting at your desk and writing one hundred wedding thank you notes without taking a break? I didn't think so! No one would, because such a task would make the writer feel overwhelmed, tired, and cranky, and such an attitude would be reflected in the notes of thanks. But you want to get those hundred thank you notes finished—I understand. Here's the secret: Break down the process of writing your thank you notes. Breaking down the writing process into smaller, more manageable chunks allows you to see and celebrate your progress while making the entire project less daunting.

If you constantly remind yourself that you have one hundred thank you notes to write, you *will* be overwhelmed and stressed. Instead, try the strategies found in *"Break It Down"* on page 26.

Remember to reward yourself when you've completed one of your thank you note writing goals, whether big or small. Do something that makes you happy. Watch a silly movie. Go out for ice cream. It's motivating to reward yourself for staying on task and reaching a goal. You're working hard—you deserve it.

Break It Down!

Task: *Finish writing one hundred wedding thank you notes.*

Break it down:

- ☐ Create a container for note-writing supplies.
- ☐ Block out time on your calendar for note writing.
- ☐ Determine what order you'll write your notes in.

Break it down even further (for example):

- ☐ Create a container for note-writing supplies.
    - ✓ Buy stamps and good pens.
    - ✓ Create a guest/gift list.
    - ✓ Place supplies inside the container and determine where to store it when it is not in use.

- ☐ Block out time on your calendar for note writing.
    - ✓ two half-hour writing sessions after dinner during the week
    - ✓ one hour of writing on the weekends

- ☐ Determine what order you'll write your notes in.
    - ✓ immediate family
    - ✓ elderly relatives
    - ✓ aunts and uncles
    - ✓ cousins
    - ✓ work colleagues
    - ✓ friends from college

Organizing Principle 5: *Systems, Systems, Systems!*

What is a system? A system is a procedure or process for obtaining an objective. For you, the objective is to create thoughtful, creative, and well-organized thank you notes for engagement, bridal shower, and wedding gifts without collapsing or having to take anti-anxiety medicine. A system will automate the mechanical steps of writing your notes and leave more room in your brain for the creative part of writing.

Having a thank you note writing system in place will help you to accomplish the following:

- *Maintain a sense of balance between your note-writing obligations and your newlywed life.*

- *Increase your productivity level.*

- *Feel refreshed, not exhausted.*

- *Spend less time thinking about and writing thank yous while leaving more time for fun and relaxation.*

- *Keep precise records. You don't want to thank Great-Aunt Gertie for her generous check after she spent three months stitching you a quilt—that's a BIG NO-NO.*

Following these five basic organizing principles will enable you and your spouse to stay focused, write your notes, and get one step closer to the thank you note finish line.

Tips for Organizing Your Time, Space, and Thank You Notes

Time

☐ Pace yourself. If you feel comfortable composing three to five thank you notes a day, then make that your goal. Don't compare yourself to any "super-brides" who claim to not sleep unless they've written at least twenty-five a day. Their lack of sleep will show in their thank you notes.

☐ Delegate! Ask someone to pick up stamps at the post office. Have your maid of honor help you compile the gift list. You do NOT have to do this alone.

Space

☐ Return the container of your writing supplies to the same spot after using it. It takes the aggravation out of trying to remember where you've left it.

☐ Give yourself ample room to write and spread out your note-writing tools. Writing is best done on a flat surface such as a desk or a kitchen or dining room table. Balancing a note card on an old issue of *Brides* magazine while watching television is not an optimal way to compose notes of thanks.

Engagement Thank Yous

☐ If a gift is mailed to you, tear off the gift-giver's return address and enter it into your address book or thank you note list (if you don't already have it on file). If neither of those is at hand, take a piece of paper and tape the return addresses to it. Once you've filled the page with the torn-off return addresses, take a moment to enter them into your address book or on your *Gift Giver Address Spreadsheet* found in Appendix E.

☐ It is difficult to estimate how many engagement gifts you will receive unless you are inviting a certain number of guests to a party. Start with a package of store-bought note cards and see how many times the mail carrier rings your doorbell before you purchase additional cards.

Bridal Shower Thank Yous

☐ At your bridal shower, have a friend or relative with legible handwriting keep track of gifts and their respective givers. You don't want to have to ask them to decipher what they wrote—they may not be able to!

☐ Have that same friend or relative use paper with lines for note taking. When the wrapping paper starts flying, it will be easier for that person to quickly jot down all pertinent information in a neat and organized fashion. They can use the *Bridal Shower Gift List Spreadsheet* found in Appendix C.

Wedding Thank Yous

☐ Your wedding guests are not the only people who may send you gifts. People who work with your mother or who went to law school with your father-in-law may send you gifts. Your former next-door neighbor may send you a gift. Remember to add these people to your wedding thank you note list if they are not already on the wedding guest list.

☐ Order thank you note cards when you order your wedding invitations. That way, you don't have to worry about purchasing them after the wedding, plus you may earn some quantity discounts.

Wedding Thank Yous *continued*

☐ Order more note cards than you think you'll need! Printing extra thank you note cards after the wedding is costly, and it can take a few weeks for the cards to be shipped to you. If fifty couples and twenty-five single people are attending your wedding, do *not* order seventy-five thank you notes (or invitations, for that matter). No matter how neat you are, you *will* need those extra cards for those infrequent spelling errors, the occasional iced coffee ring stain, and people other than wedding guests who have sent you gifts. If you end up with leftover note cards, that's great! You're now prepared to write thank yous to people who send gifts in the weeks and months after your wedding.

☐ Pack your toothbrush, your nightie, and the guest list for the wedding night. I know it sounds crazy, but if you polled recent brides and grooms to find out what they did on their wedding night, most of them (after giving you a funny look) will tell you they spent at least an hour opening envelopes and tallying their monetary gifts. Being prepared with the *Wedding Gift List Spreadsheet* found in Appendix D enables you to quickly jot down who gave you what. Take your stack of cards and your wedding guest list and fill in the blanks. It's very important to keep track of this information for when you'll be writing your wedding thank you notes.

You've grouped your thank you note writing essentials in a container and you've made an appointment with yourself to start writing. Great! You've organized the *process*. Now it's time to organize your *thoughts* and master the seven-step system to creating "crowd-pleasin'-puts-a-smile-on-their-face" thank you notes.

Ready to begin? Clear off your desktop and grab your spouse and a few good pens. You're about to discover a creative and organized writing system that will make composing nuptial-related thank yous easier than you ever thought it could be.

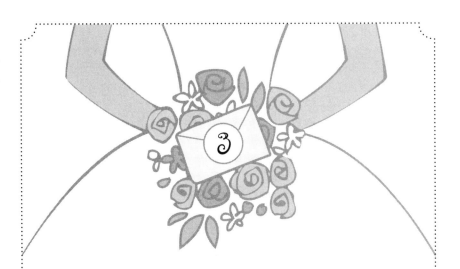

The Seven-Step System for Organizing Your Thank You Note

The seven-step system is based on the premise that a thank you note shows appreciation for a gift giver's *gift, time,* and *thoughtfulness.* Whether you're writing to your best friend, your dad's coworker, or your ninety-five-year-old great-aunt; whether it's an engagement, a bridal shower, or a wedding gift; it is important that gratitude for a gift, the giver's time, and the giver's thoughtfulness is communicated within the body of your note.

The seven steps to achieving an organized and well-thought-out thank you note are

Step 1: *Date*

Step 2: *Address the gift giver*

Step 3: *Thank the gift giver and mention the gift/its usefulness/how you are using it*

Step 4: *Attend/did not attend nuptial-related function*

Step 5: *Fond memory from the engagement party/bridal shower/wedding*

Step 6: *Pleasant ending/future meeting*

Step 7: *Sign off*

Just like any other letter, a thank you note comprises different parts. You can use all or a few of them in the body of your note, depending on your relationship with the gift giver. I have found that including all of the above components in order not only keeps my thoughts organized but enhances the quality of my thank you note as well. Here are a few examples of what you can write for each component.

Step 1: *Date*

Writing the date at the top of your note is optional. But because the recipient will probably keep your dazzling card for posterity and compare it with all other thank you notes he or she receives in the future, you may want to provide a reminder of approximately when the event took place.

Examples:

July 2013   7/13   July 8, 2013   8 July 2013

Step 2: *Address the Gift Giver*

It is most common to begin your note with Dear _____ followed by a comma. Fill the blank with the name of the gift giver. Do not draw that line or your friends and relatives will make fun of you!

Example:

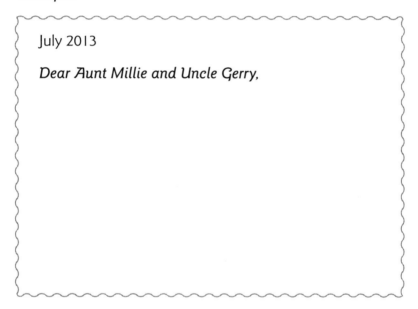

July 2013

Dear Aunt Millie and Uncle Gerry,

Be sure you have the correct spelling of all of the names of the people you are writing to. If you are unsure, call or e-mail someone who can give you that information before you start writing. It is less embarrassing to ask for the correct spelling from a friend or a relative than from the recipient of the thank you note.

Step 3: *Thank the Gift Giver and Mention the Gift/Its Usefulness/How You Are Using It*

It is very important to include a sentence or two about the gift that was given to you. This acknowledges that the gift was received and that it is making your life easier and/or bringing you great joy (which is what every gift giver wants to hear).

If Aunt Millie and Uncle Gerry gave you a blender as a wedding gift, mention it in your thank you note. This shows them that you know they made the effort to look at your registry and shop in that particular store.

Example:

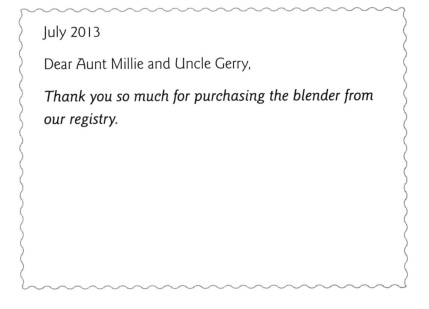

July 2013

Dear Aunt Millie and Uncle Gerry,

Thank you so much for purchasing the blender from our registry.

Everybody wants to know that their gift is one that you will use every day to enhance your married life. Regardless of whether it will actually do that, it is necessary to say so.

Example:

July 2013

Dear Aunt Millie and Uncle Gerry,

Thank you so much for purchasing the blender from our registry. *We have been using it to keep healthy by making strawberry smoothies for breakfast.*

Even if the gift is not useful or is not your taste, you must still be creative in your efforts to give thanks.

Example:

July 2013

Dear Aunt Millie and Uncle Gerry,

Michael and I would like to thank you for the silver Greek column salt and pepper shakers. Our hope is to someday take a cruise around Greece. Every time we season our food, it will remind us of you and the trip of our dreams.

If you receive cash or a check, tell the gift giver how you'll be using the money. If the gift giver is artistic, you can write that you're putting his or her gift toward decorating your new home. If the gift giver is more practical, you can tell him or her that you are using the gift to buy a new dishwasher or save for a down payment on a home. This is a thoughtful way of acknowledging the gift giver's personality and making him or her smile when reading your note.

Example:

July 2013

Dear Aunt Millie and Uncle Gerry,

Thank you so much for your very generous wedding gift. We plan on putting it toward the purchase of a very quiet dishwasher as soon as we move into our new apartment.

My advice to those who receive a highly unusual or unidentifiable gift: Have a good laugh, write a gracious thank you note, and try to sell it (the unusable gift, not the note).

Step 4: *Attend/Did Not Attend Nuptial-Related Function*

For some of your guests, the reception was a ten-minute drive from home. Others may have had to purchase expensive airline tickets, rent a car, and stay in a hotel to see you walk down the aisle. It is important to show your appreciation of their efforts and acknowledge this fact in your thank you note.

Start a new paragraph for this part of your thank you note. This breaks up the block of text and separates your thoughts.

Example:

July 2013

Dear Aunt Millie and Uncle Gerry,

Thank you so much for purchasing the blender from our registry. We have been using it to keep healthy by making strawberry smoothies for breakfast. It's now one of our most frequently used kitchen appliances!

We were thrilled you were both able to take time off from work to attend our wedding.

OR

July 2013

Dear Aunt Millie and Uncle Gerry,

Thank you so much for purchasing the blender from our registry. We have been using it to keep healthy by making strawberry smoothies for breakfast. It's now one of our most frequently used kitchen appliances!

We wish you could have been there to help us celebrate our wedding day. Your presence was greatly missed.

Step 5: *Fond Memory from the Engagement Party/Bridal Shower/Wedding*

Think about the engagement party, bridal shower, or wedding that was just held in your honor. There are often cute, funny, or sentimental moments that will stick out in your mind. Including this memory in your thank you note lets your friend or relative know that he or she was an integral part of making your wedding or wedding-related function special. If you cannot remember any, look at some pictures or watch your wedding video (if you have one). The camera has the ability to capture a moment easily missed in the excitement of an event.

Example:

July 2013

Dear Aunt Millie and Uncle Gerry,

Thank you so much for purchasing the blender from our registry. We have been using it to keep healthy by making strawberry smoothies for breakfast. It's now one of our most frequently used kitchen appliances!

We were thrilled you were able to take time off from work to attend our wedding. *You looked as if you had a great time dancing with all of your nephews at our reception.*

Step 6: *Pleasant Ending/Future Meeting?*

If you genuinely would like to correspond with or see the gift giver after your nuptial-related event, then tell them so. Start a new paragraph for this thought.

Example:

July 2013

Dear Aunt Millie and Uncle Gerry,

Thank you so much for purchasing the blender from our registry. We have been using it to keep healthy by making strawberry smoothies for breakfast. It's now one of our most frequently used kitchen appliances!

We were thrilled you were able to take time off from work to attend our wedding. You looked as if you had a great time dancing with all of your nephews at the reception.

It was wonderful seeing you again after all these years. We look forward to spending more time with you soon.

I cannot stress this next point enough: If you are *not* interested in being social with certain people after your wedding (there are always one or two), do *not* say that you look forward to spending more time with them in your thank you note. There are more poetic ways of filling the writing space of your note card. Take this advice or get caller ID, because these people will call you! It sounds mean, but it will happen.

Example:

July 2013

Dear Aunt Millie and Uncle Gerry,

Michael and I would like to thank you for the silver Greek column salt and pepper shakers. Our hope is to someday take a cruise around Greece. Every time we season our food, it will remind us of you and the trip of our dreams.

It was wonderful seeing you at the wedding. We hope you are both well and are enjoying your recent retirement from teaching.

Step 7: *Sign Off*

Your relationship with the person you are thanking often determines how you sign your thank you note. Some words and phrases that are used to close a thank you note are

Love	*Fondly*
Love always	*With affection*
All our love	*Best regards*
With best wishes	*With warmest regards*

With the sign off, all seven elements are present in your note as depicted right.

Example:

(1) July 2013

(2) Dear Aunt Millie and Uncle Gerry,

(3) Thank you so much for purchasing the blender from our registry. We have been using it to keep healthy by making strawberry smoothies for breakfast. It's now one of our most frequently used kitchen appliances!

(4) We were thrilled you were both able to take time off from work to attend our wedding. (5) You looked as if you had a great time dancing with all of your nephews at the reception.

(6) It was wonderful seeing you again after all these years. We look forward to spending more time with you soon.

(7) *All our love,* Amy and Michael

Helpful Hints for Following the Seven-Step System

☐ Create a few standard lines that you can use on multiple thank you notes. Each note does *not* have to be 100% unique. Even brilliant novelists would have difficulty measuring up to that standard.

☐ If you feel comfortable, use the same thank you note (or a slightly modified wording) for different sides of the family and friends who would never usually come in contact with each other. This works best for duplicate and monetary gifts and can be a real time-saver.

☐ When writing, use adjectives. There are hundreds of words that could and should replace overused words such as *beautiful* and *very nice*. You'll find a whole bunch of them in *Adjectives—Words that Will Move Family and Friends to Tears* found in Appendix A.

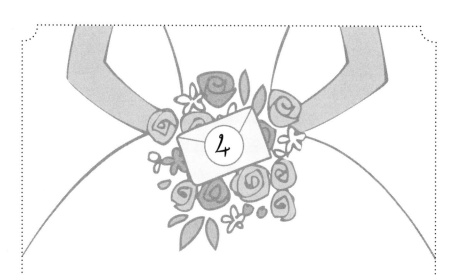

The Secret Eighth Step: Personalization

I led you to believe there were only seven steps, didn't I? Well, there are. But if you want to give your thank you note that extra "Wow!" factor, be sure to make the most of what I call the eighth step: the art of personalization.

There are two easy ways to personalize a thank you note:

  ✍ *writing with your voice or*

  ✍ *writing with the voice of the person you're thanking.*

Choose one or both to add an extra bit of thoughtfulness and personalization to your note of thanks.

Writing with Your Voice

The idea behind "writing with your voice" is to make the words of your thank you note sound as if you are speaking in person to the note's recipient.

For example, if you always say "Love ya lots!" when you say good-bye to close family and friends, end your thank you note with that phrase. People close to you are accustomed to hearing you say it, so it won't surprise but will likely charm them when they read their thank you note.

When you write your thank you notes, think of the person you are writing to. Did he wear something unique to your wedding? Did she create a gift for you from a hobby? Was he or she constantly seen smiling on your wedding video? Mention it in that person's thank you note.

Example:

> **(1)** July 2013
>
> **(2)** Dear Leslie,
>
> **(3)** Thanks so much for getting us a place setting of our china as a bridal shower gift. It will come in very handy this year since we're hosting twelve people for the holidays!
>
> **(4)** I was thrilled you were able to take time off from work to attend my bridal shower. **(5)** It wouldn't have been the same without you.
>
> **(7/8)** Love ya lots! Alice

Writing with the Voice of the Gift Giver

If you are aware of a gift giver's unique hobby, occupation, or passion or know of a certain phrase that they always use in conversation, try to weave it into your note of thanks. This concept will not necessarily apply to everyone you are writing to. You will not know some gift givers as well as others, and some people don't have a blatant characteristic that you can incorporate in their note of thanks. That's OK.

Let's say you have a good buddy from college who uses the phrase "da bomb" when describing something he thinks is great. Why not use it in his thank you note?

Example:

(1) July 2013

(2) Dear Elliot,

(3) Thanks so much for chipping in with the guys to get us that flat panel television we wanted. (8) That engagement gift is really "da bomb"! (5) We can't wait to have you all come over and watch our new DVD collection of Eddie Murphy comedies (remember *Beverly Hills Cop*?).

(6) See you at Mara's BBQ next month.

(7) Love, Michelle and Larry

By incorporating the eighth step into your system, your personalized words of gratitude will sprout even bigger smiles on the faces of your thank you notes' recipients—I guarantee it.

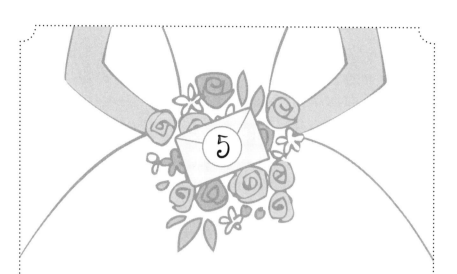

Twenty-First Century Thank You Notes: Do's and Don'ts

The bride of the twenty-first century has a few modern conveniences that brides of the past did not. Technology has enabled us to e-mail our caterers, create spreadsheets of our guest lists, and surf the Web for the perfect bridal gown. Despite the fact that most of the world is plugged in and logged on, etiquette still prevails over technology.

Every bride and groom will do what they think is best, but for those tempted to go against decades of wedding protocol, here are a few do's and don'ts for the couple of the twenty-first century.

E-Mail versus Handwritten Thank Yous

E-mail has changed the way people correspond with one another. In the not-so-distant past, one might have taken time during lunch hour or on the weekend to stroll the aisles of a local card store. Hunting for a humorous birthday card or a goofy get-well greeting was a fun and leisurely activity.

Times have changed. People are now working through their lunch hour and sprinting across aisles instead of strolling. They don't have time to look at greeting cards. They don't have time to stand in line for stamps at the post office. But they want to take a moment to acknowledge Aunt Maggie's surgery or their friend's birthday.

Along came the wonderful world of e-mail. No need to go shopping. No need to search for the nearest mailbox. From the comfort of your own desk chair, you can surf your way to well wishes and season's greetings twenty-four hours a day, seven days a week. Many websites offer free cards for popular occasions as well as occasions you never knew required a card.

Although it seems as if it would solve many issues, thank you notes sent via e-mail are not (at least yet) considered to be an acceptable way of saying thank you. Putting etiquette aside for a moment, not everyone in the world owns a computer or an e-mail account. Your Uncle Harry just got an answering machine and, to him, that is state-of-the-art technology.

Think back to when you were a child. How excited were you when a piece of mail came addressed to you? Did it make you feel special? Did you wish that you could get mail every day? Well, your wish has come true. You're now an adult and what is your mailbox filled with? Bills, junk mail, credit card offers, and donation envelopes, all addressed to you. Isn't it a great feeling to look through the stack of ordinary mail and notice that you have received a handwritten envelope? Think about how many postal workers would be out of a job if brides started e-mailing their thank-you notes!

When selecting your wedding invitations, take a few moments to look at thank you note cards as well. In many instances, you will have the option of ordering thank you notes that match your wedding invitation. If being "matchy-matchy" is not your style, you can look for note cards that instead reflect your personality or aesthetic taste. Whichever you choose, avoid using e-mail to thank those who have given so generously. Save e-mail for showing off your honeymoon pictures.

Computer-Generated Labels versus Handwritten Envelopes

The bride of the twenty-first century does not have a lot of time in her day. She is probably technologically savvy. These are two good reasons why she should print out mailing address labels for her thank you cards. Now, let me share three good reasons why she should *not* use mailing labels on the envelopes of her thank you notes.

1. *Mailing labels are a time saver. But they also show that you wanted to take a short cut to your thank yous. Remember, your thank you note is not only thanking someone for a gift, it is also thanking someone for his or her time. If people gave you some of their time, you should give them some of yours.*

2. *Your thank you notes are handwritten. If the inside is handwritten, then the outside should be, too. Consistency is key.*

3. *Businesses use labels. Personal correspondence, especially thank you notes, should not have labels slapped across the envelope. It just doesn't look good—period.*

Office Mailroom versus Pretty Stamps

You've written your note of thanks on the finest of ecru papers. In your best handwriting, you've used a pen that glides effortlessly across a page. You've sealed the envelope, and the last step is to get it ready for mailing. If you're thinking of asking the guy in the mailroom of your office to run it through your company's postage meter, don't! Stop, turn around, and march yourself straight to the post office.

Just like using mailing labels as a time saver, using a postage meter will also be seen as a short cut to the thank you note writing process. Redirect your thoughts away from the idea of free postage and pick out some LOVE or other decorative stamps for your thank you note envelopes. The stamp you choose is the icing on the cake, the final touch to your masterpiece of thanks. Creating a well-written and well-dressed thank you note with a mark from a postage meter would be like pairing a Chanel suit and handbag with a pair of flip-flops. Getting the visual, ladies?

Hiring a Ghostwriter versus Writing Your Own Thank You Notes

Many twenty-first century brides are working women who don't have a lot of extra time in their schedule. Coupled with the fact that we live in a service-oriented society, professional thank you note writing services have been created to serve a busy and exhausted post-wedding population. It may be a bride's fantasy to hire someone to write her thank yous, but there is truly no substitute for a genuine thank you note written from one's heart.

A piece of advice: If you made the time to plan your wedding, you must make the time after your wedding to thank your family and friends. If your mother finds out that you paid someone to write your thank you notes, she will have a fit and never let you forget what you did. Now *that's* more stressful than writing the notes, isn't it?

Note: It isn't necessary to reinvent the wheel with every thank you note you write. What IS necessary is to create a system for organizing your thoughts. By organizing your ideas and the note writing process, you are creating an effective way to streamline your thank you note writing responsibilities. You will have the words you need when you need them and have the note writing supplies when you need them as well.

Regifting—
Did that Really Just Happen?

No one likes to admit it, but when it comes to wedding-related events, regifting is a frequent occurrence. You're probably thinking, "My friends and relatives love me—they would never do that!" Guess again. Yes, they love you, and yes, they want to give you something that will bring joy to your married life, but they also need to purge their closets. Sometimes you won't realize that you've received a regift. It will appear to be in perfect condition and beautifully wrapped. Other times it will be blatantly obvious.

A few signs that let you know that you've been regifted:

☐ You find a card in the box addressed to "Maria on her 50th birthday." Your name is Karen.

☐ There are remnants of Christmas wrapping paper taped to the box. It's August.

☐ You recognize that vase, because YOU gave it to your neighbor as a wedding gift!

I know—you're thinking, "Cousin Shirley didn't give *me* much thought when she regifted a salad spinner for my bridal shower. Why should I spend time writing *her* a lovely card?" Repackaged, previously owned gifts, despite their lack of thought, always require a sincere thank you. After you've cleaned the regifted present and donated it, you and your spouse can share a good laugh about it.

Addressing Thank You Notes at a Bridal Shower

Asking guests to address their own thank you note envelope has been a hotly debated issue since the day someone thought of it. It is considered to be a way to give the bride-to-be a break from a portion of her thank you card writing duties. Most women are divided into two camps on this issue: One side says, "It's a game. The envelopes are used to pick names for door prizes. It also gives the bride one less thing to do during this busy time in her life." The other side screams, "Tacky! How rude to ask a guest to address her own thank you note!"

If you believe it lacks decorum to have guests do this, then subtly inform your mother/sister/bridal party of your feelings before your shower. If you're willing to take some potential heat in exchange for the convenience, then say nothing and let the chips fall where they may.

If your guests did not address envelopes but you had a large shower and you're feeling overwhelmed, have your fiancé assist you in addressing the envelopes. He's going to dry himself off with those towels and eat from those pots and pans, too. Your husband-to-be can maintain the gift list, seal envelopes, and advise you on how to thank his Aunt Sadie for her handmade toilet paper cozy. And if he wants to see you in the lingerie you received, tell him he'll need to grab a glue stick and start working on those envelopes.

Gifts Received Before the Wedding

If you research the advice given by authorities on wedding etiquette, you'll notice that most of them say that thank yous for gifts received before the wedding should be sent out before the wedding.

A recommendation from the voice of reason: Don't get all freaky, apologetic, and hard on yourself if you cannot follow the rules. Many brides-to-be of the twenty-first century have full-time jobs and are self-supporting. One month before the wedding, the modern bride's evenings are filled with appointments to firm up details with the caterer, band, florist, and photographer. Maybe she'll go to the gym one night (those last five pounds are the toughest!) and have to stay late at work a few evenings to make up for the hours spent on the phone with her best friend, fiancé, and caterer. Today's bride is not sitting around at night, pen in hand, experimenting with how "Mrs. John Smith" will look in her handwriting. She's busy and may not be able to write Cousin Matilda's thank you note until after the laundry from the honeymoon has been washed, folded, and put away.

If you receive a gift before the wedding, try your best to send out a thank you note before your wedding date. If you do not get a chance to acknowledge the gift in writing before the big day, try to go up to the gift giver during your wedding reception and thank that person for the gift. It will make the giver feel great despite the fact that a thank you note has not yet arrived in the mailbox.

Recipe for a "Crowd-Pleasin'-Puts-a-Smile-on-Their-Face" Thank You Note

- ☐ 3–5 new pens
- ☐ 1 list of gifts and people to thank
- ☐ 1 large box of thank you notes
- ☐ 1 pad of scrap paper (can substitute the back of wrapping paper)
- ☐ 1 cup of personalization
- ☐ 2 cups of love
- ☐ 2 tablespoons of graciousness
- ☐ 1 gallon-sized sense of humor
- ☐ Stamps

Clean your writing surface. Add a snack and a drink. Place above ingredients in front of you. Choose pen color. Grab a piece of scrap paper. Take a deep breath.

Start writing!

This book does not advocate going against the rules of wedding etiquette. It just advises that you do what is best for your physical and mental well-being during a joyous but sometimes stressful time in your life.

You've organized your thoughts and your thank you note writing process. You've started writing your thank you notes. That's great news! But what if from time to time you need a few creative ideas to jump-start your note-writing session? Or maybe you're writing Note No. 75 and your thoughts are starting to turn to mush? Look no further—101 sample thank you notes are just a page turn away!

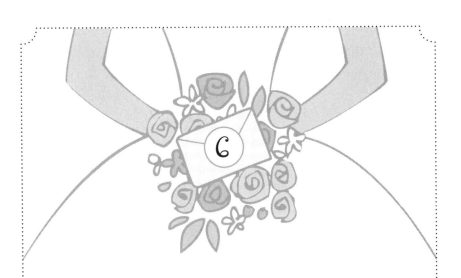

101 Modern Sample Thank You Notes

When we got engaged, my fiancé and I were blessed to receive many gifts. We knew we would be writing multiple thank you notes to the same people over the span of a year. To assist us, I looked for books offering ideas on how to thank the same people over and over without practically writing the same message. I came up short in finding what I needed: a jumping-off point and ideas to help me write numerous gracious and personalized thank you notes.

This is the book I was looking for. I wrote it for you.

I know you're busy. I know you love your family and friends and want to thank them properly for their generosity. I also think, because you are reading this book, you might want some assistance with this task. Think of these as my wedding gift to you—101 unique, creative, and modern sample thank you notes to help you reach the thank you note finish line, otherwise known as "101 ways to make your life easier and make your family and friends grin from ear to ear." Use them as you wish. Change the wording to meet your needs or don't—I leave that up to you.

Note: *Many of the 101 sample thank you notes have been written following the format of the seven-step system. Use the seven (and the eighth) steps or use just six—whatever applies to the particular note you are writing. For variety, feel free to mix up the order of the steps! They are there for you to use as a guideline.*

For quick referencing, this chapter has been organized into four categories: engagement gifts, bridal shower gifts, wedding gifts, and vendor/helper sample thank yous. Refer to each section when appropriate and scan the other sections for ideas to make your thank you notes shine. For even quicker referencing, I've created a key so you can easily find an example of what you need to thank someone for.

Thank You Note Key

- Kitchen/eating/entertaining
- Electronics
- Lingerie/boudoir
- General home
- Gift card/gift certificate/tickets
- Decorative
- Wedding/wedding-related items
- Honeymoon
- Hand crafted
- Money/stock/donation
- Support

Engagement Gifts

The ring is on your finger. You and your new fiancé have registered for china, crystal, and other household items. Before you know it, the living room is a sea of Styrofoam peanuts, cardboard, and gifts. Your new best friend is the UPS delivery person, and every corner of your home is stacked with boxes of dinnerware, appliances, and linens. The time has now come to take pen in hand and begin writing the first of many nuptial-related thank you notes. Here are twenty-five sample engagement thank you notes to get you started on your thank you note writing journey.

Physical Gifts

Dear Karen and Mike,

Serving cake on our SpongeBob SquarePants dessert platter will be a fun experience, and it will definitely liven up our table! Thank you for getting us what we think is one of the most amusing items on our registry.

Looking forward to seeing you at the next family gathering (and serving you on SpongeBob).

Love,

Dear Aunt Cynthia and Uncle Brian,

We cannot thank you enough for your very generous engagement gift. We plan on using the All Clad pots and pans to cook for ourselves as well as on those occasions that bring family and friends around our table. (Now all we need are a few of your best recipes!)

We can't wait to see you and hear all about your recent trip to New Mexico.

All our love,

Dear Carol and Scott,

Now we are ready to bake! Thanks so much for getting us the muffin tins and cookie sheets from our registry. We can only hope to create delicious desserts to rival those our grandmothers used to make!

We hope you and the kids are having a fun summer. Looking forward to seeing all of you soon.

With love,

Dear Elyse,

You got us our first place setting of china—thank you so much! Now we can have you over for dinner: We'll eat on our old dishes and you can have the Lenox!

Thanks again for getting us one of our most classic registry items. All kidding aside, we look forward to having you over for brunch. Please, please, please bring your famous cinnamon buns!

Love,

Dear Teresa, Chris, and Baby Paul,

Thank you so much for getting us the Mikasa platters we registered for. As soon as we are settled in our new place, we'll have you over for a home-cooked meal. I'll be sure to have a matching sippy cup available for Paul!

Thanks, too, for helping us with our bridal registry. We couldn't have finished it without your support and guidance.

Much love,

Dear Meghan and Mark,

Now we can serve coffee and tea with style! Thanks so much for getting us the sugar and creamer set to match our dinnerware. Hope you'll come over and help us make use of it next time you're in town (we'll provide the chocolate cake).

Thanks for thinking of us.

Love,

Dear Samantha and Ryan,

We love our new kitty cat cookie jar! We put the batteries in and now whenever one of us puts our hand in, it meows loud enough to hear it in the next room! Big thanks to you—now we'll always know who's reaching for a midnight snack.

Thanks for thinking of us and feeding our insatiable cookie addiction.

Love,

Dear Barbara and Bill,

Thank you so much for the beautiful silver candlesticks. They are a very romantic gift and will look beautiful above our fireplace. With all the work that goes into wedding planning, we look forward to taking the time to relax together by candlelight.

We hope the two of you are well. See you soon.

Fondly,

Dear Linda and Jonathan,

Thank you for the elegant crystal bowl. We fell in love with it in the store and we cannot wait to show it off—it will look spectacular in our bay window!

Thanks again for thinking of us at this special time in our lives.

Love ya,

Dear Lisa,

The handmade photo album you created for us is gorgeous—we can't wait to fill it with photos from our wedding and display it in our new home. Thank you so much for taking the time to create a one-of-a-kind piece for us in honor of this exciting time in our lives.

Hope you're enjoying your summer off! See you at Robyn's barbeque!

Love,

Dear Aunt Deborah and Cousin Ben,

We cannot thank you enough for your very generous engagement gift. The vase that you chose especially for us is lovely, reflecting the always exquisite taste of the Smith family. When we use it, our thoughts will turn to you and how special you are to us.

All our love,

Dear Whitney and Thomas,

We are in the process of selecting a wedding photographer—your picture frame is incentive to hire someone extra talented to fill it! Thank you so much for your thoughtful engagement gift.

We're looking forward to seeing you at Ken's Super Bowl party.

Love,

Dear Jenna,

What a fabulous and thoughtful gift idea! I can't thank you enough for getting us a wedding planner book. It's going to keep us very organized over the next eight months. And with all the work and research that goes into planning a wedding, I think we're going to need it!

With much love,

Dear Danielle,

You are such a creative gift giver! Thanks for getting us a wedding countdown clock. We'll have great fun watching the months, weeks, and days fly by in front of us as we plan for our big event.

Looking forward to sharing that day with you.

Love,

Dear Nicole,

We want to thank you for what could be the cutest engagement gift we received—those "I am the Bride" and "I am the Groom" t-shirts are a hoot! We wore them to the mall last week and total strangers came up to us and wished us "Congratulations!"

Your thoughtful gift definitely takes first prize for being the most creative!

Love ya,

Dear Brenda,

How did you know we both have two left feet? We can't thank you enough for getting us the <u>Wedding Day Dance</u> DVD. Now we won't look like two clods on the dance floor!

Looking forward to showing you our fancy footwork at the wedding.

Love,

Dear Skylar,

You gave me the most amazing engagement gift—the gift of beauty. Thank you for leaving work early to do my hair and makeup for the engagement party. I received so many compliments that night that I felt as if I were a model on the runways of NYC. Your talents truly shined that night!

With love,

Monetary Gifts

When thanking someone for money, do not mention the amount in your note. Instead, create a visual in the gift giver's head and tell him or her what you'll be purchasing with the gift.

Dear Aunt Eileen and Uncle Rob,

Thank you so much for your engagement gift. We plan on putting it toward the purchase of a new sofa for our apartment. We've started to look at a few and I think we agree that comfort is our #1 priority!

Thanks again for thinking of us.

With affection,

Dear Grandpa Lou,

We wanted to take this opportunity to thank you for your very generous engagement gift. With the money you gave us, we'll be able to open a special savings account earmarked for our future home. We hope to be able to someday buy a home as beautiful and cozy as the one you have.

With all our love,

Dear Aunt Patty and Uncle John,

The American Express gift check you gave us will come in very handy as we pick out furniture for our new home—thank you for your thoughtful and generous engagement gift. Now if only we could decide on a color scheme and furniture style!

Thanks again for your love and generosity.

With much love,

Dear Sari,

We can't wait to shop with our Pottery Barn gift certificate! Thank you so much for getting it for us in honor of our engagement. We're planning on using it to purchase some colorful place mats and napkin rings that match our dinnerware pattern perfectly.

As soon as we get them, we'll have you over for brunch. Jay said he'd make his famous French toast.

Love,

Attended an Engagement Party

Dear Diane and Brandon,

We were thrilled to see your happy faces at our engagement party. Many thanks to you for traveling so far to be with us as we celebrated a very exciting time in our lives. We love the hand-blown glass picture frame and can't wait to fill and display it in our new apartment. It fits the color scheme of our living room perfectly!

Love you guys,

Dear Aunt Phyllis,

Thank you so much for your thoughtful engagement gift. The "cooking for two" cookbook is going to get a workout as we shift from ordering take-out food to cooking our own meals. We were so happy you were able to attend our engagement party—it was wonderful to see you.

Love ya,

Dear Marla,

What can we say except that you are a baking genius! A million thank yous for your creativity and the time you spent creating the cake for our engagement party. People are STILL talking about it—you may be taking a few orders shortly.

Thanks again for the cake and for being the great friend that you are.

Love and frosting,

Dear Shari, Josh, and Jordana,

Thanks so much for switching your plans so that you could attend our engagement party. We couldn't imagine celebrating without you there. The monogrammed champagne flutes are exquisite—we look forward to using them to celebrate many more happy occasions together.

All our love,

Bridal Shower Gifts

The original purpose of a bridal shower was to help a new bride set up her first household. In recent years, bridal showers have also become a food-eating, game-playing, gift-wrap-tearing pre-wedding ritual.

If I offer only one tip regarding bridal shower thank you notes, it would be to have the most organized and detail-oriented guest be in charge of the gift list. Make it that person's job to write down what each guest gave you as a gift. You may be opening over 50 boxes that day; when it's all over and the guests have gone home, you won't be able to remember who gave you what. Make sure this person has neat handwriting. You don't want to mistakenly thank Aunt Becky for her tea towels instead of her tea kettle.

Here are thirty-four bridal shower thank you notes to help you thank family and friends for everything from linens to lingerie.

Dear Aunt Vanessa,

Thank you so much for getting me the decorative platter from my registry. Bob and I fell in love with it and can't wait to use it when entertaining family and friends.

Thanks too for helping Mom transport the balloons. Mom's car is barely big enough to fit her and Dad! I hope you had lots of fun at my bridal shower.

Much love,

Dear Lucy,

Sending you a big bowl of thanks for getting me the cookbook written by my favorite TV chef. Dave and I are looking forward to making many meals together, and this cookbook should help me get over my fear of boiling water!

See you soon!

Love,

Dear Grandma Sylvia,

Thank you so much for the huge soup pot—it reminds me of the one you always made chicken soup in. I hope to be able to fill it with homemade soup that tastes as good as yours.

I was thrilled that you were able to travel to my bridal shower. It meant a lot that you were able to be there to celebrate with me.

I love you very much.

Dear Gail,

I wanted to thank you for taking the time to peruse our registry and select the only item that Adam wanted—the nonstick wok! He and I enjoy stir-frying and we'll be ordering less take-out food and spending more nights cooking together in the kitchen after the wedding.

Thanks again for your gift (and Adam thanks you, too)!

Love,

Dear Helen,

Thanks so much for the Mickey Mouse teapot. It's going to look adorable on our stovetop. After the wedding, we'll have you and Michael over for tea and yummy pastries.

It was lovely seeing you at the shower. Ted and I look forward to celebrating with you and your hubby at our wedding.

Love,

Dear Lynn and Rita,

I'm going to be baking up a storm thanks to you! I love, love, love the red stand mixer that now is the centerpiece of my kitchen counter. I've already made a cake for Sam and he can't wait for the next one!

Thanks, too, for helping Mom set up the buffet at the shower. I heard the task took longer than anticipated, and I am so appreciative that you jumped right in to lend a hand.

Much love,

Dear Evie,

Your recent trip to Japan must have given you a great gift idea. Thanks so much for putting together that spectacular sushi-making gift basket for us. Everything we'd need for making sushi was included—right down to the wasabi and pickled ginger!

We can't wait to buy some sushi-grade tuna (our favorite) and use our new sushi tools.

Love and chopsticks,

Dear Anne Marie,

Thank you for the Brita and three-pack of filters. Peter and I prefer water to most other beverages and we can't wait to start using it. It's going to come in very handy—especially after we come back from our nightly jog!

Best wishes and happy new year!

Love,

Dear Karlene,

Thanks so much for getting Phillip and me the food processor from our registry. We love to cook! Not only will your gift speed up our food prep time, it will help us to prepare more complicated recipes and give us more "together time" in the kitchen.

Happy holidays! See you soon.

Love,

Dear Aunt Olivia,

Doug and I are not morning people, so we'd like to thank you for helping us get up and start our day. The coffee maker you selected is perfect for us. We can set it the night before and the smell of coffee fills our home to get us moving in the morning.

I'm so glad you could be at my shower. Thanks for taking all of those pictures—I'm going to have albums full of wonderful memories.

Love you,

Dear Leanne,

The hand-painted pitcher you gave us won't be empty
for long! Thanks so much for indulging an iced-tea
junkie with a beautiful way to serve drinks. It will
be a terrific addition to our decorative serving piece
collection.

Thanks also for helping my mom clean up at the end
of the shower. We both really appreciated your help.
See you at the wedding!

Love,

Dear Andrea,

Thanks so much for getting us the oval platter that
matches our dinnerware set. My specialty is chicken
piccata and boy, is it going to look scrumptious on
that platter! We'd love to have you over one day so
you can see for yourself (and eat the chicken, too,
of course).

See you at the wedding!

Love,

Dear Paige,

I love to make homemade soup—thanks so much for the three-speed hand blender. Putting it directly into the pot is going to save me a great deal of time when it comes to pureeing and cleaning up. I've always seen chefs use it on TV, and now I'll be able to make soup as easily as they do!

Hope you had a fun time at my shower. Dig out your dancing shoes—the wedding is just around the corner!

Love,

Dear Sarah,

Just wanted to drop you a note of thanks for your heart-healthy shower gift. Dan and I plan on spending many nights preparing meat, fish, and veggies on our new indoor grill. I think we'll be eating more meals at home now that we have such a terrific cooking tool!

As soon as we get our apartment settled, we'll have you over for a barbeque.

Love,

Dear Morgan,

Thanks for introducing me to the wonders of the ten-piece nesting bowl set. I just started using it and I can't begin to tell you what a fabulous kitchen tool it is. I don't think a day goes by that I don't use one of the ten bowls from the set—and they take up almost no room in our cabinet. We have a small kitchen so the less space an item takes up, the better!

Thanks for such a useful and organized gift. I hope you had an enjoyable time at the shower!

Love,

Dear Noreen,

Our dinner table will have great pizzazz thanks to your colorful shower gift. The tablecloth you picked out matches our dinnerware perfectly. We can't wait to have people over so we can start using it. Please tell us when you're free for brunch!

Thank you for your thoughtful gift.

All my best,

Dear Yvonne,

Thanks so much for the decorative ice bucket and matching tumbler set. The Hawaiian theme was the perfect choice for us since we'll be honeymooning there. At least you'll know that whenever you come over, we'll always be ready to offer you a cool drink in a cool glass!

It was great seeing you at my shower. I was so glad you could make it.

Love,

Dear Lindsay,

Thanks to you, there's a lot of chocolate-dipped food in our future. The fondue set you gave us will provide us with many a yummy dessert and hopefully not too many post-wedding pounds! We'll have to have you over so we can break it in.

You bring your empty stomach and we'll provide the dippables! Mmmmmm...we're getting hungry just thinking about it!

Love,

Dear Aunt Fran,

Thank you so much for your fun and creative shower gift. Justin and I LOVE ice cream—the ice cream maker and dish set will provide us with hours of fun and hopefully not too many extra calories!

We look forward to seeing you and Uncle Norman at the wedding.

Love,

Dear Carley,

Mitch can't wait to make boatloads of chili for our annual Super Bowl party in our new crock pot. Dinner and party preparation will now be a snap thanks to your thoughtful gift.

Also, many thanks for helping carry all the gifts to my mom's van. I think without your help, we'd still be dragging them across the parking lot!

Much love,

Dear Aunt Bess,

Nelson and I love to cook together and we wanted to thank you for the 20-piece Tupperware set you gave us. It provides us with a way to keep our healthy and home-cooked meals fresh and well organized in our refrigerator.

Hope you're ready to dance at our wedding—see you in a few weeks!

Love,

Dear Hillary,

Many thanks for getting us the '50s-inspired toaster from our registry list. Our kitchen is going to be decorated in 1950s kitsch and the new toaster will fit in perfectly with the décor. We're also addicted to Mom's homemade jam, so we plan on toasting everything from multigrain bread to English muffins.

Looking forward to seeing you on the big day!

With warmest regards,

Dear Sandy,

Brunch will now be a gourmet meal in our home—
thanks so much for the Belgian waffle maker. As
soon as we master the maker and eat some practice
waffles as quality control, we'll have you over for a
midday feast.

It was great seeing you at the shower—get ready to
party at the wedding!

Love,

Dear Angela,

Thank you for the apron and matching oven mitts.
They're sure to add a splash of color to our kitchen
and we'll be well protected against high heat and
flying spaghetti sauce!

I hope you had a fun time catching up with the
family at my shower. See you at the wedding!

Love ya,

Dear Collette,

Thanks so much for getting us the BIGGEST SALAD BOWL I have ever seen! There will be no problem having crowds over for meals now that I own the biggest salad bowl this side of the Mississippi. Two of my friends have already asked to borrow it for their family reunions!

I'm thrilled you were able to take a few hours out of your busy work schedule to celebrate with me.

Love ya lots,

Dear Christie,

Boy, did I blush when I opened your gift! Thanks so much for the gorgeous bra and panty set. I know someone who will love it as much as I do...

I'm so glad you were able to take time off to be at my shower. See you at the wedding!

With love,

Dear Melissa,

What can I say about your "Wedding Night" theme gift? I really do love it but Bruce loves it even more. He keeps reminding me to pack it in my bag for after the wedding!

Thanks for your creativity and for adding some unexpected excitement to my bridal shower.

Is that why we're called "blushing brides?"

Love,

Dear Aunt Estelle,

What a great shower gift! Jack and I love to go on picnics, and the picnic basket and bottle of wine you gave us will work beautifully when we go to hear concerts in the park.

Thanks so much for thinking of us—there will always be room on our picnic blanket for you.

Love,

Dear Wendy,

Thank you so much for getting us monogrammed towels for our master bathroom. We love the personal touch and can't wait to wrap ourselves in them!

Besides your generous gift, I can't thank you enough for coming to my shower. I'm sure it can't be easy to get away for a few hours when you have a new baby at home.

Much love,

Dear Julia,

Thank you for getting Ian and me a gift card to Crate and Barrel—we just LOVE that store. We've been up and down the aisles many times and already have a few things in mind that will look great in our future home.

We'll see you at the wedding!

Love,

Dear Felicia,

I cannot thank you enough for your gift of pampering.
The certificate for a one-hour massage is a gift that
I will cherish as the day of my wedding quickly
approaches. I think I'll schedule my appointment for
a few days before the wedding so I can rid myself of
all party-planning stresses!

Thanks again for a much-needed gift.

Love,

Dear Aunt Dale,

Thank you so much for getting Noah and me our
bed-in-a bag set. We fell in love with it when we saw
it and now we can't wait to have cozy nights under
our new comforter. Boy, is it going to be tough to get
out of bed in the morning!

We're looking forward to seeing you and Uncle Abe
at the wedding.

With love,

Dear Michelle,

Charlie and I can't thank you enough for getting us a few important items for our honeymoon. We're going to look through the guidebook to Hawaii while we lie on the beach on our new monogrammed towels. What a fantastic gift!

Mahalo (look, I'm already speaking Hawaiian)! See you at the wedding!

Luv ya,

Dear Aunt Pearl,

A suitcase full of thank yous go to you and Uncle Artie for getting us the two pieces of carry-on luggage we registered for. Their first trip on an airplane will be for our honeymoon (I'm sure they won't mind traveling to Aruba!).

We share the same love of travel as you and Uncle Artie do, and we look forward to packing our new bags and taking time to explore the world as a married couple.

All our love,

Wedding Gifts

You've finished writing your bridal shower thank you notes. Congratulations! Take a few weeks off from thank you note writing—the arrival of the first wedding gift is just around the corner! Yes, some of them will arrive before the wedding. Most of them will arrive at and after your wedding. But don't panic!

Here are forty-two different ways to say "thank you" to your loved ones and the people who helped make the day as beautiful as it was.

Physical Gifts

Dear Marlene,

Thank you so much for your unique wedding gift. The decorative bowl will not only come in handy for parties but will also bring a burst of color and chic styling to our dining room table.

We hope you had a fun time at our wedding. We were so happy you were there to celebrate with us.

Love,

Dear Isabel and Gary,

Thank you for your beautiful wedding gift. It was so sweet of you to think of us. We've used the woven ceramic basket many times while entertaining, and it has served us well as a fruit bowl and for holding bagels. It even reminds us a bit of our basket-weave-patterned wedding cake!

We saw you whooping it up on the dance floor! We're glad you had a good time at our wedding and were able to join us at the last minute.

Love,

Dear Cousins Dana and Aaron,

We were so excited to receive your wedding gift! Thanks so much for getting us a 25" TV for our den. And just in the nick of time, too! Our 15-year-old set from Uncle Burt's apartment just played its last news broadcast two days ago.

It was great being able to hang out with you at our wedding. Can't wait to have you over to watch the World Series on the new TV!

All our love,

Dear Uncle Harold,

We can't thank you enough for the DVD player and DVDs you got us as a wedding gift. Now we can have you and the rest of the family over for movie night. We'll make the popcorn!

It was great to see you at the wedding. Wishing you continued good health.

Love,

Dear Cousin Rachel,

We'd like to thank you for your very generous "can't wait to spend it" wedding gift. The gift certificate to Home Goods will come in very handy as we transform our apartment from former bachelor pad to cozy home for two.

It was great seeing you at the wedding—let's play "catch up" at Aunt Sally's 65th birthday party.

Love,

P.S. Thanks for fixing the bustle on my gown after the ceremony. You were a lifesaver!

Dear Joe and Patrice,

Thanks so much for helping us complete our Crate and Barrel registry. We love their products and were so excited to receive the goodies that we had on our list. Our personal favorite is the set of veggie-themed dish towels—perfect for our kitchen!

We were so delighted to see your smiling faces as we walked down the aisle. We look forward to being there to share in the joy for the two of you next year!

All our love,

Dear Emma and Alexandra,

What a heavenly wedding gift! We cannot begin to thank you for the gift certificate for a couples massage at the Om Day Spa. It was a luxury on our wish list and now you made our wish come true!

We were so happy to see you at our wedding and we look forward to seeing you at the next Sawyer Family gathering. We'll be very relaxed next time we see you!

Love,

Dear Aunt Harriet,

What can we say about the handmade quilt you created for us? It is stunning, and the fact that you made it with your own two hands makes it extra special to us. Thank you, thank you, so much!

Your generosity and kindness to us over the years has provided us with a constant source of happiness. We always enjoy spending time with you and we look forward to celebrating many more happy occasions together.

With much love,

Monetary Gifts

Dear Jackie,

We want to take this opportunity to thank you for your very generous and thoughtful wedding gift. The contribution you made to our online cash registry enabled us to have an unforgettable day of sailing while on our honeymoon in Hawaii. It was gorgeous there!

And thanks for sending Mom a stack of pictures from the ceremony. She hasn't stopped showing them to her friends! Talk to you soon.

Love,

Dear Abby and Brent,

Thank you so much for your wedding gift. We plan on putting it toward decorating our home—now if only we could agree on how to decorate it!

We hope you had a fun time at our wedding and that it brought back fond memories of your own recent walk down the aisle.

Love,

Dear Uncle Frank,

We were thrilled to see you on the dance floor at our wedding—we hope you had as much fun as we did that day.

Many thanks for your generous wedding gift. We will be using it to create a beautiful home together as husband and wife. When we finally unpack all the boxes and make our place livable, you must come over for a visit!

With much love,

Dear Connor,

When spring comes, we'll be putting your wedding gift toward the purchase of some backyard furniture. Thanks for helping to give our family and friends a place to sit while they eat their hot dogs! Being two former apartment dwellers, we suspect that this shopping trip will prove to be an interesting experience!

It was great to see you at the wedding. As soon as the patio set arrives, you can have your pick of burgers or hot dogs.

Love ya,

Dear Penny and Anthony,

Thank you for your generous wedding gift! We're adding it to our furniture savings account and hope to use it to buy a bedroom set. It's a good thing John and I both like Mission-style furniture or else we could still be shopping for a bedroom set as we take our first child to college!

It was lovely seeing you at the wedding and we hope to see you again soon.

Love,

Dear Cousins Jane and David,

We can't thank you enough for your wedding gift. We are thinking of using it to purchase a new dishwasher. With all of the new dishes and pots we now own, we're going to need one!

We heard through the grapevine that you really enjoyed yourselves at our wedding. We're so glad you came and we look forward to catching up with you at the next cousins get-together.

All our love,

Dear Melanie and Steven,

We are very appreciative of your generous wedding gift. It won't be long before we're able to use it to purchase furniture for our new home—we have our eye on a cozy loveseat for two!

We hope you had an enjoyable time at our wedding. We were both glad you could make it and share our special day with us.

Love,

Dear Judy and Zach,

Thank you for your generous wedding gift. We plan on using it to buy a cool and unique piece of artwork for our new home. Now if only we could see eye to eye on what's cool and unique!

We hope you had fun at our wedding and look forward to seeing you again soon.

Love ya,

Dear Josephine,

We were so glad you could come to our wedding. We hope you had an enjoyable time on our special day.

Thanks so much for your wedding gift. We're going to put it toward the sugar bowl and creamer that match the teapot you gave us as a shower gift. Then we'll really be able to entertain with style!

We'll have you over for that pot of tea soon. A box of English Breakfast will be waiting for you—we know that's your favorite.

Love,

Dear Lonnie and Fred,

We would like to thank you for your very generous wedding gift. We plan to use it to finish purchasing our dinnerware collection so we can entertain and not have to use paper plates anymore!

We hope you had a great time at our wedding—we were thrilled to have you there. Looking forward to seeing you at the next holiday gathering.

Best regards,

Unable to Attend Wedding

Dear Julie,

We wanted to thank you for the adorable chip and dip set you sent us. It came in very handy when we had friends over to watch the Oscars, and we've used it many times since then.

We are so sorry you were unable to be with us on our wedding day. Your cha-cha expertise was missed on the dance floor! We hope to get to see you next time you take a vacation up north.

Best wishes for a happy and healthy new year.

Love,

Dear Janine,

The three-footed pitcher was a hit at our last family get-together. That pitcher sure can hold a lot of lemonade! Thank you so much for your lovely wedding gift.

We were so sorry you were unable to attend our wedding. We wish you could have been there.

Thanks again for thinking of us on our special day.

Love,

Dear Uncle Tim,

We were so sorry you were unable to attend our wedding. We hope the next time you fly into town we'll be able to get together and show you our wedding album.

Thank you for thinking of us. Your gift will help us save for and create a relaxed and inviting home together as husband and wife.

We hope you are feeling better. Best wishes for a speedy recovery.

Love,

Dear Aunt Carolyn,

Thank you for your thoughtful wedding gift. It was sweet of you to send us a ceramic candy dish and think of us on this important day in our lives.

We were sorry you were unable to attend our wedding—your presence was greatly missed. We hope you are well and enjoying the great weather Arizona has to offer.

With much love,

Unique Gifts

Dear Robyn and Tom,

Words fail to express how excited we were to receive your creative wedding gift. The Hinman Playhouse is only a short drive from our home and the two-year subscription you gave us will provide much entertainment and a good excuse to have many a date night.

We were so happy you were able to share our wedding day with us. Thanks again for one of the most creative wedding gifts we received.

Love you,

Dear Jeff,

We're going to tell your mother she got her money's worth out of sending you to art school! The painting you created for us in honor of our marriage is breathtaking. It is a gift with considerable meaning—one that we will treasure for a lifetime. Now we just need to find the perfect spot for it!

Thank you from the bottom of our hearts for taking the time to create a one-of-a-kind piece of artwork in our honor.

All our love,

Dear Roseanne,

How many ways can we say thank you to someone so talented? Your hand-crocheted afghan has kept us warm on chilly nights and goes perfectly with our new bed linens. It was a very thoughtful gift and one that we will always cherish.

Also, many thanks for keeping Mom calm during the wedding planning!

With much love,

Dear Jordan,

Thanks so much for helping us to post all of the pictures from our engagement party, shower, and wedding online. Because of your thoughtfulness, we were able to share our special occasions with people who could not join us in person.

If any of our engaged friends need the same assistance, we will gladly pass your name on to them!

Love and JPEGs,

Dear Matthew,

Now we _really_ know how much you like soda! Thanks so much for giving us a very generous wedding gift of ten shares of PepsiCo stock. We've been thinking about creating a stock portfolio as a married couple, and this was the perfect gift to help us get started.

No more store-brand soda for us!

With love and fizz,

Dear Aunt Barrie and Uncle Lance,

We cannot thank you enough for your thoughtfulness and generosity. Making a donation in our name to the American Cancer Society in honor of our wedding was the perfect way to include Grandpa Jack in our special day. We missed his presence but we know he was with us in spirit.

With much love,

Traveled to Come to the Wedding

Dear Jill and Todd,

Thanks so much for traveling a great distance to come to our wedding. It meant so much to have all of our cousins around us on our special day.

We love the martini glasses and barware and look forward to using them when hosting future celebrations. Rob makes the best appletini! Next time we gather, he'll have to show off his bartending skills.

Love,

Dear Monica,

Thank you for your thoughtful gift and for traveling so far to see us walk down the aisle. It meant so much to us that you were there to watch us take the matrimonial plunge. The Macy's gift card is the perfect gift for us. We have our eye on a few different sheet sets—now if only we could make a decision!

We hope you had a fun time at the wedding. Next time you're in town, we'd love to have you over and show you how cute you looked in the wedding video!

Love,

Dear Aunt Nancy and Uncle Jerry,

Thank you so much for your very generous wedding gift and for traveling many miles to share in our special day. We can't wait to use the Bloomingdale's gift certificate—we have our eye on a beautiful comforter that will blend perfectly with our new paint colors and keep us toasty at night.

We're looking forward to seeing you on our next trip out West.

Love,

ora,

*...e way from London you came! We were so
...ited to hear that you had a business meeting in
our city the weekend of our wedding. Thank you
so much for your British-inspired gift basket and for
making the time to join us on our special day. I've
already started using the Harrods tote the gift
came in!*

*It was great to see you and hear your newly acquired
accent!*

Cheerio,

---

*Dear Aunt Ellen, Uncle Ray, Randi,
and Owen,*

*We wanted to thank you for your generous wedding
gift and for traveling many miles to be with us on
our wedding day. Seeing your smiling faces made us
smile too as we walked down the aisle.*

*Our plan is to put your gift toward our dream of
creating a home as comfortable and inviting as
yours. You are very important people to us and we
love you very much.*

Hugs, kisses, and love,

Dear Anna and Kevin,

We wanted to take a moment to thank you not only for your generous gift card to Target but for the love and support you showed us as we made our wedding plans. Coordinating vendors and selecting a honeymoon spot would have been a challenge without your wise input, experience, and opinions. We hope to be able to pay it forward in the future.

All our love,

Dear Cassie,

How do we begin to thank you for offering to provide all of the candles for our wedding? The colors and scents you selected were the perfect accents to our flowers and reception décor. Everyone was talking about how beautifully the candles lit up the room! Thanks so much for your generosity and for making our wedding an illuminated experience for all.

Love and tea lights,

Dear Sean,

Thanks so much for videotaping our wedding. We just finished watching the video and were amazed at your great composition skills and your ability to capture moments that we missed entirely. The cake gets eaten, the band goes home, and what we're left with is the video and our memories. We can't thank you enough for the gift of fond memories that you so generously presented to us.

All our love,

Dear Mrs. Johanson,

We'd like to thank you for your generous gift of doing the calligraphy for our wedding invitations. Betsy kept telling us about how very talented you were and she was right—your handiwork speaks for itself. I hope you get to start your small business soon. When you do, I'll be sure to send my engaged friends and family members right to your doorstep.

With much thanks and appreciation,

Dear Tara,

We just wanted to send you a note of thanks for singing at our wedding. All of the cousins have said that you have a beautiful singing voice, and they were right. We got to dance our first dance as a married couple to what sounded like the heavens parting and an angel serenading us.

Thanks for all of your hard work and for making our wedding day so unique and special.

Love,

Dear Patrick and Fabian,

We wanted to drop you a note of thanks to tell you how much we love our wedding pictures. Through the magic of photography, you managed to capture the feelings of love and excitement that blanketed the day (and you made us look fabulous in the process!). Whenever we show our wedding album to people, they always "oooh" and "ahhhh" over the beauty of the photos.

We were very pleased with your work and we plan on passing your business card along to all of the engaged couples we meet.

With gratitude,

Dear Martha,

You must be a fairy godmother because I truly felt like a princess on my wedding day!

I just wanted to say thank you to the most talented dressmaker I know and for accepting the challenge of creating the dress I would wear when I walked down the aisle. From fabric selection to the tiniest of details, you were there with pincushion in hand to design the most gorgeous gown I have ever laid eyes on. Thanks to you, I felt incredibly beautiful and graceful when I got married.

With all of my love and appreciation,

To the Best Maid of Honor,

Sierra, I can thank you a thousand times, but it still would not be enough to cover all that you did for me as my maid of honor. From the moment I asked you to be my maid of honor to the moment you left us at the airport for our honeymoon, you were a great source of fun, strength, and support. And you're so organized! Wedding planning would not have gone as smoothly as it did without your ideas and input. I am most grateful for all you did and hope to be able to do the same for you someday.

With lotsa love,

Dear Denise and the staff at Elegance Caterers,

Our taste buds are still tingling from the three-course meal you created for our wedding day. Our parents can't stop talking about the salmon entrée, and three of our friends asked if you would give away your recipe for the stuffed mushrooms passed around at the cocktail hour! Your waitstaff was professional at all times, and the food was presented with great style. We are most appreciative of all of your efforts.

Thank you for making our wedding day as special as it was. We will gladly give your name out to anyone we know who is planning a party, big or small.

All our best,

Appendixes

Appendix A

Adjectives—Words that Will Move Family and Friends to Tears

Adjectives can work wonders for a thank you note! Here are words to help you describe the gifts you have received:

A: adorable, aromatic, attractive, awesome

B: beautiful, big, billowy, bright

C: cheerful, classy, clever, colorful, colossal, comfortable, cool, creative, cuddly, cute

D: dashing, dazzling, delicate, delicious, delightful, dynamic

E: elegant, enormous, excellent, exotic, extraordinary

F: fabulous, fancy, fantastic, flawless, funny, fuzzy

G: gigantic, gleaming, glistening, glorious, gorgeous, graceful, grandiose, great

H: handsome, hard-to-find, heavenly, helpful, hilarious, huge, humorous

I: imaginative, immense, impressive, incredible, interesting

J: joyous

K: kind

L: lavish, lovely, lucky, lush, luxurious

M: magical, marvelous, modern

N: natural, new, nice, nifty, numerous

O: outrageous, outstanding, overjoyed

P: perfect, precious, professional

Q: quaint, quick

R: ritzy, romantic, royal, rustic

S: sentimental, sexy, shiny, silky, silly, smooth, soft, sophisticated, sparkling, special, spectacular, spiffy, splendid, subdued, super, superb, supreme, swanky, sweet

T: tasteful, terrific, thankful, thoughtful, tranquil, tremendous

U: unique, useful

V: valuable

W: warm, well-made, whimsical, wild, wonderful

X: X-rated

Y: yummy

Z: zany

*Here are words to help you describe
family, friends, or services:*

A: amazing, accommodating, appreciative, artistic, attentive, awesome

B: brilliant

C: calm, caring, clearheaded, considerate, creative

D: dedicated, dependable, devoted

E: easygoing, efficient, elegant, eloquent, encouraging, energetic, entertaining, enthusiastic, excellent, extraordinary

F: fabulous, fantastic, fun

G: gentle, genuine, generous, good, gracious, great

H: helpful

I: impressive, ingenious, inventive

K: knowledgeable

L: lively, lovely

N: nice

P: passionate, pleasant, priceless, professional

R: reliable, remarkable, responsible

S: saintly, satisfied, sincere, sophisticated, speedy, superb, sweet

T: talented, terrific, thoughtful

U: understanding

V: versatile, vivacious

W: wise, wonderful

Feel free to mix and match the adjectives on these lists for your needs, or take out your handy-dandy thesaurus. Yes, the one you used in high school—go dust it off. The thesaurus is one of the best places to find words that sparkle like jewels. If you're on your computer, consult an online thesaurus for determining the right word for the right sentiment.

Gift Lists

Appendix B - Engagement Gift List

Appendix C - Bridal Shower Gift List

Appendix D - Wedding Gift List

Appendix E - Gift Givers' Address List

Gift lists are an easy way to inventory every gift you receive and check off your thank you notes as you write and mail them.

Date	Engagement Gift Giver

the organized bride's thank you note handbook

Engagement Gift Description	Note Written	Note Mailed

Date	Engagement Gift Giver

Engagement Gift Description	Note Written	Note Mailed

Date	Engagement Gift Giver

Engagement Gift Description	Note Written	Note Mailed

Date	Bridal Shower Gift Giver

Bridal Shower Gift Description	Note Written	Note Mailed

Date	Bridal Shower Gift Giver

Bridal Shower Gift Description	Note Written	Note Mailed

Date	Bridal Shower Gift Giver

the organized bride's thank you note handbook

Bridal Shower Gift Description	Note Written	Note Mailed

Date	Wedding Gift Giver

Wedding Gift Description	Note Written	Note Mailed

Date	Wedding Gift Giver

the organized bride's thank you note handbook

Wedding Gift Description	Note Written	Note Mailed

Date	Wedding Gift Giver

the organized bride's thank you note handbook

Wedding Gift Description	Note Written	Note Mailed

Date	Wedding Gift Giver

Wedding Gift Description	Note Written	Note Mailed

Date	Wedding Gift Giver

the organized bride's thank you note handbook

Wedding Gift Description	Note Written	Note Mailed

Bride	Groom	Gift Giver

Address

Bride	Groom	Gift Giver

Address

Bride	Groom	Gift Giver

the organized bride's thank you note handbook

Address

Bride	Groom	Gift Giver

Address

Bride	Groom	Gift Giver

Address

About the Author

Stacey Agin Murray is a professional organizer located in Fair Lawn, New Jersey. Her company, Organized Artistry, LLC, was born in 2002 out of the desire to help others on their journey to an organized life.

Stacey's formal education includes a BA in art/graphic design from the State University of New York at Binghamton and an MA in art education from Teachers College, Columbia University. Stacey's informal education includes growing up in a 5' × 12' bedroom (smaller than some jail cells!) and mastering the art of making the most of her horizontal and vertical space. She actually thought her college dorm room was spacious!

Over the years, Stacey has contributed her organizing knowledge and expertise to periodicals such as *(201) Bride, Reader's Digest,* and *Working Mother Magazine* and was a columnist for *Organize Magazine.* She has also contributed to websites including SheKnows.com, Learnvest.com, and iVillage.com. She has appeared with expert organizer Peter Walsh on Oprah Radio—an unbelievably fun experience Stacey will never forget!

She is a member of the National Association of Professional Organizers (NAPO), NAPO's Golden Circle, and the New Jersey Association of Women Business Owners.

For more information and to read Stacey's blog, go to organizedartistry.com. Sign up for the Organized Artistry newsletter to get her useful, helpful and profitable 'Top Ten Tips for Organized Living.'

Connect with Stacey on Facebook and Linkedin and check out Organized Artistry's organizing and wedding boards on Pinterest.

For more information, please contact
Stacey Agin Murray
Organized Artistry, LLC
PO Box 2682, Fair Lawn, NJ 07410
(201) 703–8438
stacey@organizedartistry.com
organizedartistry.com